STORY

Learning to Forgive

With Compliments from:-

Christian Focus Publications
Geanies House
Fearn
Tain, Ross-shire

© Glenn Myers
ISBN 1 85792 287 5
Published in 1997 by
Christian Focus Publications, Geanies House, Fearn,
Ross-shire, IV20 1TW, Great Britain
and
WEC Publications, Bulstrode, Gerrards Cross, Bucks,
SL9 8SZ, Great Britain
Cover design by Donna Macleod

Contents

Introduction

The first time I met Cathy Church she was sitting one row in front of me in a meeting. She wore her waist-length blonde hair in plaits, a thing I had not seen since schooldays, and I was tempted to give them a playful tug and see what happened.

When she got up to speak, I thought fleetingly of Pollyanna: five foot nothing in flat shoes, a young, pretty face, freckles, green eyes, a slight lisp.

Then she started unfolding her story. She found Jesus in the midst of her own broken home. Still a young woman, she had been working for God in some of the unhappiest places on earth. She spent two years among Vietnamese boat people in the Far East. Then, she brought medical care and the Christian gospel into the simmering ethnic hatreds in Sri Lanka, at the tip of the Indian subcontinent. With the Sri Lankan work over, she was about to leave for Cambodia: the land where a million people had died in four short years and where landmines, poverty, epidemics, and a shattered infrastructure have kept the nation, and an infant church, reeling in shock.

I wanted to tell her story from that day on. She was not an easy person to track down, even by letter. When we were doing this book, Cambodia had one telephone for every thousand people, and

Cathy was one of the other nine hundred and ninety-nine. Mail had to be sent to Thailand from where it was carried over the border once a week. Faxes only took 30 seconds to get to the WEC office in Cambodia but then several days passed before they reached the remote northern province where Cathy worked. And, anyway, for weeks on end she could disappear up the Sekong river, a tributary of the Mekong.

"You could always come over," Cathy told me. (I was based in nearby Singapore.) "It's quite safe, so long as you don't use the roads." Eventually, over a period of two weeks in Singapore, I got to interview her at length.

Cathy's story is mostly about suffering: about pain, about not being able to cope, and about the slow struggle to love people whom you actually hate. But it is also about how God can bring us through all these things and cause us to bear good fruit for Him. As Cathy said, "God commands us to forgive and love. And He doesn't give commands without also giving us all we need to keep them."

1: 'Daddy's girl'

"I hate you!"

Cathy Church glared at her reflection in the bathroom mirror. The green eyes staring back at her were full of loss.

It was a Sunday morning in April, 1975, the day before her fifteenth birthday.

Cathy had been raised in Kentucky. From the age of nine, she remembered the bickering and shouting that had violently consumed her mum and dad's marriage, like flames in a timber house, and had forever scarred a little girl's world.

After the divorce, her mum took Cathy and her two sisters to Florida, where she remarried. Cathy's stepfather loved his bride with tenderness. The household they built was happy – with one exception. Her new daddy began to abuse Cathy, the little girl who was his middle stepdaughter.

Now, tension crackled whenever he and Cathy came near each other. It took almost nothing to have them yelling. Cathy was sneered at, shouted at, and – when Mum was not around – physically hurt. She hated him, dreading the times, especially the nights, when they were alone together in the Florida home.

Family photos show Cathy sitting apart from the others, already marking herself as the family reject. At high school, unlike her sisters, she chose the worst companions, the shortest skirts, and the wildest dates. She insists she was not driven to any of this by her home circumstances: it was her choice. But nothing delivered what she thirsted for – a father's love.

That morning in the bathroom, feeling sick, seeing herself in the mirror, and not knowing what she had done the night before, or who she had done it with, her life scraped bottom. She was the only one of her sisters with a taste for drugs and abusive boyfriends, the only one who stirred cruelty in her stepfather. It was unreal. With teenage logic she decided she was some kind of monster.

* * *

That Sunday morning, this same teenage logic suddenly made Cathy decide to try religion.

She called Jan, a neighbour who was a few years older than Cathy and her friends, and a girl they had already relegated to oddball status. Jan drove Cathy to the little Church of God building that evening.

Cathy recalls what happened:

"That night, I heard clearly that God loved me. And to me that was the most amazing thing because I felt like nobody loved me. I was a horrible person.

"I knew that I kept doing terrible things and I couldn't stop myself. I wasn't in control any more ... To find out that the Almighty God, the Creator of the Universe, loved me, was the most marvellous, unbelievable thing. And so that night I gave my life to the Lord."

Over the next weeks she peeled off some of the dead layers of her life. The drugs and drinking went. So did the wild, empty dates. She got a new bunch of friends, the young-adult group at the church. Called 'Abba's children', many had about the same degree of weirdness as any previous Cathy Church date. But they were hungry to know and love God.

Abba is the first, stumbling word the Hebrew toddler uses for his daddy, the intimate name for God that Jesus used. Cathy was happy to call herself *Abba's woman*, Daddy's girl. Her life changed so drastically that within a month, Pam and Ruth, her two closest girlfriends, became Christians too.

* * *

The alleycat fights with her stepfather did not change straightaway. They still swapped high-decibel curses, he still poured beer over her head, and she still hated him.

Outside the home, Cathy started having more

fun than she had had for years: every weekend would find her water-skiing, picnicking, or camping with 'Abba's children'. Cathy, Pam and Ruth were the babies of the group, and they were finding quality friendships, with people who cared for them, and who modelled the Christian life for them. It was an intensely happy period for Cathy, growing in Jesus, having fun, loving and being loved.

The faultline in the landscape was her lonely fight with her stepfather, and the guilt she felt for loathing him. Everything she tried failed: staying out of his way, keeping quiet, trying not to retaliate, resolving to be better, praying. Untouched by the other changes in her life, these underground strains kept shaking her new happiness to pieces.

One night they had a huge fight and her stepfather flung a heavy lamp at her. It missed. Cathy screamed something back at him and then slammed the door on the way out of the house. She hitchhiked over to Jan's place.

Tears were streaming down her face as she spilled out her thoughts to her friend: "I can't be a Christian! You can't be a Christian if you don't love people ... and I hate my stepfather ... I don't just dislike him ... I *hate* him!" To Cathy's black-and-white mind it looked like the chains of a life she could not escape were still wrapped tight.

Jan tried to help. Cathy was right, she explained, about the Bible's statements on hate. The person who persists in hate does not, cannot, know God. But she was misunderstanding Christ's ways of love.

"Jan told me," Cathy recalled, "that love is a commitment, not a feeling. I had to make a commitment to treat my stepfather in a loving way, no matter what he did to me and no matter how I felt."

Jan and Cathy prayed, and Cathy made a commitment to act in a loving way, by returning insult with kindness, humiliation with patience; overcoming evil with good – even if she felt hatred in her heart.

As they prayed, heaven seemed to open briefly: "A tremendous amount of love came down upon me," Cathy said, "And I know that it was of God, it wasn't me."

Cathy's home life was not the same after that night. She and her stepfather still had major-league fights, and Cathy smouldered with hurt. Sometimes she still wished him a horrible death but, as she sought to obey God, she was finding new resources in her heart:

"Each new time we fought, there was a strength. The word of God says that the Holy Spirit is our Comforter and I felt like the Holy Spirit was walking with me through it. I felt He was going to help me through each of those situations: that He was going to give me the courage and the ability to be able to love my stepfather."

It took several years, and leaving home for nursing school in Atlanta helped, but slowly the storms between them did subside. The two alleycats lived in peace, even affection. Cathy began to feel love in her heart for her stepfather, despite everything he had done.

Her stepfather responded. When she needed to upgrade her car for the frequent trips between Atlanta and Florida, he added enough money to buy a new one, a wonderful surprise. And once – only once – he managed to tell her that he loved her.

* * *

At the same time something else was happening in Cathy's life: a growing sense of being set apart for God's service. At a Jesus festival in 1976, Cathy heard a speaker, Ann Kiemel, talking about how to share the good news about Jesus with others. Offhandedly, Cathy said to some friends, "If God gave me a gift of love like that woman has I would go anywhere He asked me to go."

That night another speaker stopped in the middle of his address and said to the huge crowd, "Someone has asked God for the gift of love. God is giving you that gift." One of Cathy's friends nudged her. "That's for you," she said.

"I'd forgotten I'd said that," said Cathy.

She felt more and more that God wanted her to serve Him full-time overseas. When she applied for nursing school in Atlanta, the form had a question about her expected future career. In her curly childlike handwriting she wrote, firmly, 'Missionary Nurse'.

One evening, in the middle of a church service, she began to feel God's presence beside her in an overwhelming way. She knelt down, worshipping and praying, not caring what was happening around her. Then she heard God speak to her audibly.

He told her not to worry about trying to convert her family — they would all find the Lord in time. (Both her mother and her natural father did indeed turn to Christ before they died.)

God also promised that He would use her 'in a mighty way'. Even today, Cathy will not talk about other promises made at that time; but they became like bedrock in her life.

* * *

One June day in 1983 Cathy spent half a day in prayer, sitting under her favourite tree in the local park. She was praying about her missionary calling and felt 'very strongly impressed' that it was time to move on. Not only that, but she felt that God was going to move her on before the end of September. She wrote all this down in her diary.

A few weeks later she watched a television show sponsored by the Christian relief agency World Vision and called the phone number at the end. World Vision explained they did not need nurses at that time, but gave her the number of a similar group, World Concern. It turned out that this group had a vacancy for a nurse to work among Vietnamese Boat People in a refugee camp in Malaysia.

Cathy plunged into a flurry of prayer, consultations with her pastor, and application forms. For a month or two it was an on, off, on-again, will-she-won't-she time that was only bearable because of the peace that filled her heart.

The goodbyes said, she boarded the plane to World Concern's headquarters in Seattle, Washington. On the plane she fished out her diary; it was the last day of September.

2: Among the Boat People

Less than three months after finding Malaysia on the map for the first time, Cathy arrived, in 1983, aged 23. It was her first time out of the United States and her luggage took a connecting flight somewhere else.

Stories of the Boat People filled the world's television screens in the early 1980s. Fleeing Vietnam in ramshackle boats, those who did not drown were washed up in their thousands in countries like Hong Kong, the Philippines, Malaysia, Singapore and Thailand.

Unwelcome wherever they beached, Boat People were sometimes pushed back out to die at sea. Most were herded into refugee camps. Here they waited, sometimes for years, for the chance of a new start, usually in Australia, Canada, the United States, or Europe.

The Sungei Besi Holding Center, a few miles from Kuala Lumpur, the capital of Malaysia, was a well-run camp: little corruption, reasonable food (even if it was the same every day), no riots, and – unless you were chronically sick, a proven liar, or a known communist – quick at processing the people who passed through. Most Boat People flew out to new homes within a year of their arrival.

The United Nations paid for food and clothing

for the refugees. World Concern – the Christian agency that had recruited Cathy – ran the medical programme from a collection of creaky trailers. Cathy worked alongside a couple of other nurses and a Filipino doctor.

* * *

The boy whom Cathy met in sickbay one morning a few weeks later had sores all over his sparrow body. He was lying on the bed, silent and still, with his face towards the blank wall. His name was pronounced "Yum", and he was 10 or 11 years old.

He had sailed from Vietnam with his mother, father and brother. A normal voyage took seven days. Yum's had lasted more than seven weeks. The boat had been repeatedly attacked by pirates.

The first pirates raped Yum's mother. A second pirate boat took all the women, including his mother, and he never saw her again. They also plundered everything from the boat, including the engine.

The rickety craft drifted helplessly in the ocean until attacked for a third time. Angry that there was there was nothing left, the pirates murdered the grown men, including Yum's father, and threw them over the side.

The children left on the boat had no food or

water, and Yum had to watch his brother slowly die. Finally, rescuers sighted the boat and pulled it in.

Cathy stared down blankly at Yum for a few seconds, then walked out into the back room in the sickbay and shut the door behind her.

She had already been told his case history and realised she did not know what to say to Yum, or how to start caring for him. Nothing in all her nursing experience had prepared her for this. She breathed a prayer: "God, I can't do anything for this boy ... I'm completely inadequate."

"*That's right*" – she felt God saying to her – "*You are.*"

The back room was quiet except for the muffled sounds of the camp outside: children playing, people talking and laughing as they walked past.

"*You* are *inadequate. But I can work through you.*"

Cathy explained, "I've never forgotten that. I am inadequate. There's nothing I can do. I don't have any special abilities. I don't have anything to give. But God does...

"I think that throughout all of my ministry that's the thing that has characterized my life. I can't do anything. But it's the most wonderful place in the world to be, because when you're inadequate and can't do anything, that's where God can do it. That's when God can move."

Cathy walked back into the ward.

"I didn't do anything grand. I cleaned his dirty body and took care of him and held him in my arms when he would start to scream and cry."

Yum's story started a new chapter some months later when a Canadian Christian family heard of him and opened their home to the orphan.

* * *

Cathy lived with World Concern colleagues in an apartment in Kuala Lumpur. Six days a week, a bus would collect them, grind through the outskirts of the city into Sungei Besi town, and then on to the gate in the double-fenced enclosure of the refugee camp.

Settled into her medical routine, she started a couple of Bible study groups in the camp. She also set up a club for eighty Vietnamese children, which quickly became the highlight of her week with songs, a story, games, and crafts.

Many of the children had never heard of Jesus Christ. When Cathy asked once if anyone had a something they wanted to sing, one newly arrived six-year-old gave Cathy a military salute and suggested a Viet-Cong communist song!

* * *

As in refugee camps all over the world, displaced Vietnamese were open to change and many turned to Christ. Ten-year-old Huang was Cathy's shadow, helping at the children's club and running errands. After becoming a Christian, she led her whole family to Christ.

Sickbay had a constant turnover of Vietnamese helpers. At Christmas, four months after Cathy's arrival, the two Vietnamese girls who worked as interpreters became Christians. Most of the people who helped in sickbay and came along to the Bible studies eventually did the same, as did many other adults and children.

A few months after Christmas, Cathy was introduced to two beautiful women in their early twenties, Anh and Hong, who were to be the new interpreters for the medical centre.

Like many of the people in the camp, these women had faced unimaginable danger. Their boat too had been subject to pirate attack. Fearing rape and murder, Hong had cried out to Jesus. (Some of the refugees had a Catholic background.) Miraculously, the pirates had not touched Hong or her sister Anh. Finding Cathy talking about the same Jesus at Sungei Besi, Hong became a Christian practically straight away.

But not Anh. She worked as Cathy's personal interpreter for some months and came along to the Bible studies. In sickbay, she was sensitive and caring. Always polite and gracious, she gently refused all invitations to shift her allegiance from Buddhism to Christ. Cathy longed for her to change her mind and receive the Lord.

"During the time Anh was my translator," Cathy remembers, "maybe five, six months – I was going through a very difficult time. I was discouraged. I was feeling very lonely. I was feeling like a failure. I was losing my temper a lot.

"I was coming home almost every night and crying out to the Lord, 'Why did you bring me here? I'm doing more harm for your gospel than good, because I'm being such a terrible witness.'

"And then the next day, even though I would get up saying I was going to be better ... I was just getting depressed and angry. I felt like I was a complete failure as far as being a missionary was concerned."

In time, Canada accepted Anh and Hong's application for refugee status. They were due to leave while Cathy was in the United States for a couple of weeks' leave. On the last evening before Cathy's trip Anh asked Jesus to be Lord of her life.

Shyly she explained why. "Cathy, I know you've been going through hard times in the past few months, and I see how Jesus has helped you through. When I leave the camp, I'm going to have hard times. I want the same Jesus to help me."

"Here it was again," Cathy remarked. "I'm failing but the Lord was using my failures for good, for Him."

* * *

At the church she attended in Kuala Lumpur, the young people's drama group tried ever more ambitious projects: skits in the shopping centres, a musical, special presentations for Christian festivals, visits to the refugee camp. Cathy was invited to help with the Sunday School teaching ministry in the 1,500-strong congregation. And she spent regular time one-to-one with new Christians.

She spent hours working with the church drama group for an Easter festival, gloomily convinced they were not going to be ready. Come Good Friday, 1,500 sat through the young people's performance. Eight hundred more came on Easter Sunday evening, many watching with tears in their eyes. Once again Cathy, who saw so many faults in her work, was surprised that God could use it.

* * *

At the end of her two-year commitment to World Concern, Cathy wanted one of two options:

either to live in the camp and work completely among the Vietnamese, or to work in Kuala Lumpur where she could serve in the local church.

When neither option opened up, she decided it was time for something new. In 1985 she flew out of Malaysia, back to the United States, and began working out what to do next.

3: The Land of Serendip

Colombo, Sri Lanka

Riots [occurred] between Tamils and Sinhalese last week in Trincomalee, a predominantly Tamil town on the east coast. Six people died and 2,000, mostly Sinhalese, were left homeless.

Time magazine, 12 October 1987 – three months before Cathy arrived.

Finding out what to do after leaving Malaysia and the Boat People meant a more winding road than Cathy expected. Following the advice of her pastor, Cathy looked at serving with her denomination, the Assemblies of God.

Months passed. When nothing seemed to be happening, Cathy's pastor suggested she try some other missions. She selected five from a list. She explained, "I sent applications to each organization and said, 'Lord, whichever one responds positively, I'll see that as You opening the door.' So, of course, all five of them responded positively!"

Worldwide Evangelization for Christ (WEC) was the slowest.

"They were really slow. But when they finally wrote back, what impressed me was that I clearly saw they had taken my letter seriously and the headquarters staff had prayed before writing a positive response." Cathy's pastor, too, was keen. And so she started the four-month orientation course to join WEC.

"The only problem was that I wanted to go back to Asia, and WEC wanted me in Africa. I prayed and prayed about it. I thought I was supposed to go with WEC and so I left it to the Lord to work it out."

By the end of the orientation course, Cathy had her plans all fixed to go first to Europe and after that to West Africa. Then she came across a paper written by a WECer in a country called Sri Lanka, a teardrop-shaped island in the Indian Ocean.

A handful of WECers worked in Sri Lanka, all seconded to other organizations. Jobs were available for missionary nurses. Cathy spoke to the WEC leader in the United States. They prayed and fasted, and decided that Cathy should go to Asia after all.

Cathy had a long, year's wait for a visa. She spent the time speaking at college meetings across America and working with the children's ministry in her church. It was September 1987, when she was aged 27, before Cathy got her first breath of Sri Lanka's steamy, curried, tangy air.

* * *

WEC's five-foot-nothing new recruit arrived in a jewel of a country that was flawed to its heart by long years of ethnic strife.

Sri Lanka means 'The resplendent land'. The Arabs called it Serendip, a place of unexpected, wonderful findings. It is an apt name for a land of rubies, sapphires, and starstones. In the jungle and wasteland that cover half of the island you can come across elephants, deer, leopards, boars, jackals, monkeys, cheetahs and buffaloes. In the centre are ruined cities that flowered two thousand years ago with temples taller than Egyptian pyramids.

Most people in Sri Lanka are Sinhalese, devout Buddhists originally from North India. Most of the rest are Tamils, from South India, who are largely Hindu (with some Christians). You can also find Muslims, descendants of the Sufi trader-missionaries who spread Islam all round the coastlines of Asia and Africa.

Like ethnic strife around the world, the Sinhalese, Tamil and Muslim conflict in Sri Lanka is ancient, bloody and complex. The current wave of violent death started in 1983 with the murder of Sinhalese soldiers by the Liberation Tigers of Tamil Eelam (LTTE), the so-called 'Tamil Tigers'. The Tigers claim to be fighting for independence for the Tamil area in the north-east of the Resplendent Land.

* * *

Cathy was initially seconded to an indigenous evangelical aid organization, though she later worked directly for the Government. They sent her to be the nurse in charge of a refugee-camp clinic in the coastal town of Trincomalee.

The town sits on a finger of land overlooking just about the best natural harbour in Asia, a strategic port fought over and occupied in turn by the Portuguese, Dutch, French, and British. If the Tamils ever got their homeland it would probably become a border town. Trincomalee sits on the fringe of the Tamil area and its 50,000 people belong almost equally to the three main groups, Tamils, Sinhalese, and Muslims.

In the latest round of rioting, three months before Cathy arrived, Tamils had burnt and looted Sinhalese homes, creating refugees by the thousand. Most of these people were now housed inside a military base called Fort Frederick, in huts hastily built from *cajun*, the dried local palm leaf.

Fort Frederick was a castle built and buttressed by generations of European military. Perched on a peninsular, it was accessible only by a winding road guarded by a thick stone gateway. Cathy was the only trained nurse for 10,000 displaced Sinhalese, most in this camp, the rest in smaller camps nearby.

Cathy was shown a two-room house which she was to share with five Sinhalese girls, rural health workers with the Sri Lankan equivalent of the Red Cross. In the room they all used as a dorm, Cathy had a space for her mattress and a similar-sized space for her things; everything else was shared. Only one other girl spoke any English. "It was," Cathy remarked, "a good way to learn Sinhala." As lifestyles go, it was an intense one: lonely but rewarding.

Cathy explained: "Living with people of another culture is very difficult, especially if you don't speak the language, and they don't speak English.

"You're putting yourself into a very vulnerable position, where the people that you're living with are the experts, they are the educated ones, they are the people that know everything. And you are a nobody. Like a child, you can't speak, you don't even know where to go to the bathroom. You have to ask about everything. You're an idiot.

"But that somehow opens up the people to develop relationships that they never would if you were the teacher and they were the student. They teach you about the culture. They correct you. They look after you. They open their homes to you.

"So it's very difficult, it's very humiliating, there are lots of times when I've spent time crying and screaming and angry, especially at not being able to make myself understood, or being misunderstood, or because I have nobody to talk to, nobody to help me through things.

"But it also throws me back onto God. And He's supposed to be my best friend. He's supposed to be my lover. If I'm always depending on other people to fill these needs then I'll never depend on God."

* * *

Cathy found five or so newly born Christians among the thousands of Buddhists in her camp, and met with them to praise God and pray together. Sinhala takes a year or two for a Westerner to learn even when you are not in a clinic all day. In their first meetings, Cathy found that communicating with God was fine, but communicating with the others got little further than smiling and saying "Hallelujah".

The only regular times she got to be alone were the hour she spent with the Father each morning, on the fortress wall overlooking an empty beach; and the one week in four that she spent resting at the WEC base in the dust and clatter of Colombo, 120 miles to the south west.

* * *

Month by month, the *cajun* huts in the shade of the banyan trees slowly emptied. As looted and burnt areas of Trincomalee were made safe again, the Sinhalese were able to leave Fort Frederick, return to their homes and start rebuilding. Slowly, the tension in the air eased.

Outside the camp Cathy found opportunities to serve the Tamil Christians. The Tamil churches were excellent, well-led, indigenous and growing. They were also sinking under the weight of suffering around them. Many members struggled with the pain of the ethnic fighting; many had lost their livelihoods. And other refugees – often misfits who were neither fully Sinhalese nor fully Tamil – were everywhere knocking on church doors seeking help.

* * *

Throughout Cathy's first three years in Sri Lanka, the situation was easing and the Sinhalese refugees were going home. Working with the Ministry of Health, Cathy began to do clinics in Muslim villages. After twelve months, she left Fort Frederick, and moved in with a Christian Tamil family in Trincomalee, where she savoured the luxury of a room to herself.

The ever-changing political situation seemed to have brought some kind of peace. For a while, everyone could move around Trincomalee and ethnically different neighbours were friends.

Cathy, or *Sudu aka* ("white elder sister"), was well-known in all the communities in Trincomalee, which was, despite all its bloodshed, only a small town.

Cathy was becoming fluent in Sinhala; she was settled and happy in her ministry; and she had good friends in all the ethnic groups. The hardest stage of her ministry in Sri Lanka seemed to be over. And it looked like the land was finally getting some rest from war.

It looked that way right up to 11 June 1990.

4: "That was a riot"

A thousand people are feared dead over the past four days in fierce fighting between Tamil Tiger guerrillas and Sri Lankan security forces....

With no prospect of a ceasefire ... the fighting spread to the coastal town of Trincomalee in Eastern province. While helicopter gunships and naval gunboats attacked rebel positions, the guerrillas used mortars and rockets in their attacks on the three Army camps, at Kiran, Kalmunai and Kalawanchikudi in the east...

The Times, London, 15 June 1990.

What happened on 12 June 1990 no-one exactly knows.

It started as a normal day. Cathy went to work in Fort Frederick. In the afternoon she attended an opening ceremony. The Trincomalee Women's Welfare Organization was inaugurating a small manufacturing plant. The workers were all widows and the plant was going to make up packets of a vitamin-enriched food supplement for children.

Jan, an expatriate working with the Save the Children Fund, gave Cathy a ride home in her car. It was just getting dark. As they clattered through Trincomalee they heard the pop-pop-pop of gunshots. Jan asked Cathy if she wanted to spend the night at her house, in a safer area on the other side of Trincomalee, and with a car in case they needed to leave in a hurry. Cathy said no, she was fine. Even in peacetime, it was not unusual to hear shooting in Trincomalee.

Cathy shut the car door, waved goodbye to Jan, and went into the house of the Tamil family with whom she lived.

Doy and her husband were closing the shutters. Baby Josie, born just 17 days earlier, lay sleeping on a mat; two-year-old Roshanthan sat on the clay floor beside her. The family from next door, close relatives, had joined them. For greater safety they all moved to Cathy's room, at the back of the house, where they waited for the shooting to stop, as it usually did.

Sitting on the floor to avoid stray bullets, they heard shells and bombs exploding. Josie woke and fed, snug at her mother's breast. The shooting got louder and more frequent. "It might be the army practicing and firing shells into the sea," someone said.

Roshanthan was sleepy and excited at the same time, dozing between bomb-blasts. The adults sat and waited, some silent, some talkative. "It doesn't sound like practice," said someone else. The sounds of war got nearer, a few streets away.

"Sometimes they fire into the air as a warning."

Suddenly two shells landed almost on top of

the house with a huge, deafening explosion. The house rocked and the electricity blew out. A few moments later, stones and heavy debris clattered onto the tin roof.

They lit an oil lamp and calmed the children. Cathy fetched her torch. They argued over what to do. Some were for leaving; others wanted to sit it out. None of the options was pleasant.

At about two o'clock in the morning the gate in the fence rattled. No-one moved. It kept banging and behind it someone was calling out. Finally one of the men got up and slowly opened it.

At the gate was a young boy, a so-called "Tiger Tail", who worked for the Tamil Tigers. He was carrying a message: the Tigers were attacking the town. Everyone had to leave and go north, deeper into the Tamil area.

North was the last place Cathy wanted to go. She would have preferred to return to the town centre, or to the army camp, or to the Save the Children Fund home. Or south, out of Trincomalee district altogether. Her Tamil family did not have those options.

They quickly packed up some food. Doy took baby Josie. Cathy, who had a man's bicycle, put a little pillow on the bar so that little Roshanthan could sit on it and lay his head on the handlebars. Then the father got all the bags and food and put that on another bicycle.

It was dark outside the house. Sometimes Cathy could not see her hand pushing the bike because the air was so full of dust from the shelling.

Everyone was leaving and the dark street was swollen with people and noise. She kept glimpsing the crowds in the flashes of light from exploding shells. People were shouting back and forth. "Do you know where so-and-so is?" "Have you seen my sister?"

Cathy knew the people in a Methodist church in Nilavali, about six or seven miles north along the coast road. That would be safe: she fixed the thought in her mind as she pushed the bike with one hand and kept hold of Roshanthan with the other.

They trudged through the crowded night. In the dark they sometimes passed people bleeding from shrapnel or bullet wounds. It was almost unbearable for Cathy to have to walk past them and not help.

Some of the teenagers around were laughing and joking. Cathy wanted to scream. "What are you laughing at? Don't you know what's happening?"

They walked all night.

* * *

Day was breaking and they were very near Nilavali when they saw a car nosing towards them.

Two Sri Lankan men were in the front with two white ladies in the back. Cathy flagged it down. The ladies were French tourists from the nearby Nilavali Beach Hotel. They were being driven to safety by their tour guides. Were they going to Colombo? Yes, eventually. Could Cathy have a ride? Yes, jump in.

She had a stressful conversation with her family in the middle of the crowded street. She did not want to leave them: it felt like betrayal.

"No, you must go. You're one less person for us to worry about. You're one less mouth to feed."

She wanted to take the children and get them out to safety, but the parents refused. Finally, reluctant to be separated, she hugged the children and climbed into the car.

* * *

Aching, tired, hungry and grieving, Cathy wanted to put her head under a blanket and never come out again. Happily, the French women spoke very little English and so, after some stabs at conversation, Cathy did not need to talk.

They drove south, through the crowds of Tamils. In the gathering daylight, they saw smoke, burning buildings, and empty houses. They passed Tamil checkpoints, and then army checkpoints, only getting through because they were foreigners.

When they finally drove out of Trincomalee

province, it was suddenly another world. In the bright sunshine, children, neat in school uniforms, lined up to start classes for the day. Shops and markets were open. Old cars, trucks and motorbikes spluttered and smoked, filling the streets. It was as though Cathy had just left the cinema   after watching an all-night disaster film.

* * *

Safely out of the war zone, the French ladies wanted to continue their guided tour.

This was almost more than Cathy could take. She was deep in shock, not knowing if she would ever see her Tamil family again. The Army would be looking for her, the stray foreigner. So would the people from Save the Children Fund. She needed to get down to the WEC base in Colombo, five hours away, and tell the authorities where she was.

The Sri Lankan drivers offered to drop Cathy off at a bus station. This was the normal way she travelled but today she could not bear the thought of slow grinding journey and all the people asking questions.

So she sat quietly in the car while they visited Sri Lankan tourist sites. You can find plenty of attractions between Trincomalee and Colombo if you are prepared to detour. The Sigiriya citadel, for example, a palace perched on top of 600 feet of red rock, with Asia's oldest landscaped garden dug out of the jungle at its base. The sacred Bo tree in Anuradhapura's ruins, an unlovely stump tended continuously by gardeners through 23 centuries. You can see lots of dagombas, the pudding-basin-shaped cathedrals of Sri Lankan Buddhism. The French ladies snapped their photographs.

They reached Colombo in the twilight, twenty four hours after the shells had started thudding into Trincomalee's suburbs. The Sri Lankan drivers found Cathy a trishaw to take her to the WEC base.

* * *

At the WEC base, Nancy, who regularly provided Cathy with hospitality, was not expecting her.

"I didn't know you were coming today! I haven't got you a bed ready or anything!"

Cathy was about to collapse.

"Nancy, I couldn't tell you beforehand. I didn't know war was about to break out."

5: Ashes

For two anxious weeks, Cathy fretted in Colombo, wondering about her Sri Lankan family and trying to get back up to Trincomalee. Daily she phoned Save the Children, the Army, the Health Ministry, anybody she could think of. Fighting was still going on, but finally she got clearance to travel up with Jan, who had also been evacuated safely, and join in the relief effort.

They drove up in the Save the Children Fund vehicle. Their first sights of Trincomalee were shocking. At least a third of the houses in the town were looted and damaged. Many had been burnt to the ground.

The Tamil Tiger attack on Trincomalee had completely, and inevitably, failed. The Sinhalese retaliation had been a bloody outpouring of hate and violence against every Tamil in the town. Almost every Tamil house had been broken into and looted. Tamil businesses and shops were destroyed. Only the churches, temples, mosques, and some of the houses owned by Tamil government officials had been left intact.

As Cathy and Jan drove around, finding out what the relief needs were, they learnt that the largely-Sinhalese Army had almost finished 'clearing' the town. This innocent-sounding term meant that soldiers had searched all the Tamil areas for weapons and arrested most of the able-bodied men. Camps had been set up for the Tamils left behind. These camps, often inside religious buildings, provided food and water as well as protection. Once an area was pronounced cleared, the refugees were free to leave the camps and start rebuilding their homes.

Cathy and Jan met a number of women in the camps who had been raped during the rioting. Others frantically pleaded for news of husbands or sons who had vanished into the night.

Cathy finally found some of her neighbours. They told her that Doy, Josie, Roshanthan and the rest of her family had survived the riots and were staying with relatives in Trincomalee. Cathy drove past their empty house: it was still standing but looked like someone had broken into it.

* * *

On her second day in Trincomalee, Cathy drove back to her house through the deserted streets, to found out if anything of hers had been damaged. She was a friend of both Sinhalese and Tamils and, because she lived simply, she did not think anything would be stolen. With her natural optimism she hoped that one way or another her room would have been spared.

Cathy felt weary and sick as she opened the

door of the silent house. It had not been spared. Half of the roof at the back was blown off, everything inside was smashed, and food littered the floor.

She trod through the debris to her room and pushed the door open. Everything she owned was gone. "That was," Cathy said, "the straw that broke the camel's back."

"Everywhere I'd been," she explained, "it had only been the Tamil houses that were burnt down. A few, but not many, Muslim houses. The Sinhalese houses were not touched. It was always the enemy's houses.

"So when I saw that they'd violated me, taken my things, all of a sudden, I knew, had been placed on the side of the 'enemy'.

"And I hadn't done anything to deserve that. That's when it really struck me. That's when the fuse came down to the dynamite and I blew up."

The Sinhalese who had looted the house were people she knew: her friends, people whose babies she had delivered, people she had joked with on the streets, people who had opened their homes to her, people she had eaten with, people who had affectionately called *Sudu Aka*, 'white elder sister'.

These people, whom she had loved and prayed for, had emptied her room and stolen things that were treasures only to her. They had treated all she was and everything she had done for them with total contempt – all because she was living with a Tamil family.

She told me: "I completely lost trust in the Sinhalese people." Anger against them filled her heart.

* * *

Outside the town, the refugee situation was critical. Outlying districts needed family food parcels, water pots, and chlorine to clean out the wells. Cathy joined in the government-led relief effort, working alongside the handful of Save the Children Fund and Médecins sans Frontières (MSF) volunteers.

It was not just physically hard work. Everywhere, they met grieving Tamils. Occasionally they saw places where bodies had been burned in the streets. And they discovered it was impossible to be seen as neutrals.

Cathy explained: "What happens when you try not to take sides is that everyone says you are on the opposite side. So, even though I was not pro-Tamil and not pro-Tigers, the Sinhalese thought I was a Tiger supporter."

The higher ranking Army officers knew and trusted her; but on the ground the accusations flew, no matter how silly: Tamil sympathizer, CIA agent. Sometimes humanitarian aid was delayed by Army personnel who suspected that the relief workers were smuggling it to the Tigers.

For Cathy it looked as though all her care and love for the Sinhalese, painfully built up through the years, had been reduced to ashes along with much of Trincomalee.

"When the Sinhalese were refugees," Cathy said, "I worked with them for three years. Now, all of a sudden, the Sinhalese were not in need any more. The Tamils were in need. So I was trying to help the Tamils. But I was being accused and rejected by the Sinhalese.

"And the Sinhalese were the people whom I really wanted to serve. The Tamils already had good churches. And there were wonderful, well-grounded Christians who were strong believers among the Tamils. But my heart was with the Sinhalese. Because they were the group of people who had not heard the gospel, who needed to hear. It was these people who were slapping me in the face. They were the ones who stole from me. They were the ones who were accusing me falsely. They were the ones who were spreading rumours about me."

* * *

Through the ever-reliable Trincomalee town gossip network, Cathy found out within a few days where nearly all her stolen goods were. All she wanted back were two suitcases, gifts from her sister, that were full of personal things.

As soon as her schedule permitted, which was not very soon, Cathy and her Tamil landlady, Doy, went over to Fort Frederick. They wanted to see the Colonel, the senior army officer who had been responsible for Cathy's safety during the year she had lived in the fort. He was a person of integrity and Cathy knew he trusted her.

Fort Frederick was full of victorious, happy Sinhalese: some with the Army or local government, some coming for shelter from the fighting, and some who were still refugees from the riots-before-last.

Cathy and Doy walked through the fort to the government buildings which were cool under the shade of banyan trees. They passed through a crowd of Sinhalese, most of whom Cathy knew personally.

"Most of the Sinhalese wouldn't look at me," Cathy said. "Everybody knew what had happened." A few greeted her shyly: none had much to say; many avoided her completely.

The Colonel did his best, but he could not do much – he still had a war to fight. He called the police, told them Cathy was coming, and ensured she would be treated properly.

"It was perhaps unrealistic," Cathy admitted,

"to think that these high-up officials could do anything about one little person's belongings."

She reported the thefts to the police. Behind the counter, the bored policeman took her list. He was a Sinhalese, like almost everyone in the security forces.

"We'll do what we can," he said, not looking her in the eyes and not looking like the list was going to go much further than the nearest waste basket.

"They knew where the things were," Cathy said. "Everybody knew where they were. *I* knew where they were. Through the gossip network you could find out where all the looted goods were."

Controlling her voice the best she could, she told the policeman, "I had two brand new suitcases, gifts from my sister, that had personal things in them. I don't care if you don't get my stereo back. I don't care if I don't get my other things back. There are no two suitcases like this in all of Sri Lanka, and you know where they are, and that's all I want back."

"Nothing," Cathy told me, "was ever returned."

* * *

Two weeks later Cathy had to leave Trincomalee for the annual WEC team meeting in Colombo.

6: "A high and difficult walk"

WEC team meetings, at their best, are a time to catch up on news, relax, worship, listen to God, discuss goals, evaluate progress, and make decisions.

In 1990 the WEC team in Sri Lanka was just three single women and one couple, all of them recent arrivals. They did not have a developed leadership and pastoral care structure. Instead, Ken Booth, who with his wife Cecily had responsibility for advising all the WEC teams in South Asia, oversaw the work. Ken had flown in for the meetings.

It was not a great conference. "I was," Cathy said succinctly, "an absolute snot."

She could not eat. Nor could she control herself when they tried discussing other people's problems. "Your dog's been sick! Well at least your dog's alive and not dead like half the parents of children up in the war area ..."

She did not feel she could share her pain. She would say enough to shock and hurt, and then retreat from their efforts to help.

"I was afraid that if I shared too many things," she explained, "they would get upset, and that was not what I needed. I wasn't so depressed, or sad. I didn't need to cry. I needed to shout. I was angry. There may have been some tears but they would have been tears of anger and frustration."

At the end of the conference, the team urged Cathy to stay in Colombo for a while. Ken suggested she got advice from Helen Roseveare, a veteran WEC missionary who had suffered rape and imprisonment in the 1960s during a violent uprising in what is now Zaïre.

"The main healing," Cathy said, "came from sitting down and writing that letter to Helen, and then getting the answer. When I poured everything out in my letter, that was basically my only outlet ... there just wasn't anybody else, except the Lord, and that is a very difficult place.

"I don't know why God put me in that situation, but I know He gave me the grace to handle it. God would have provided an outlet if He'd wanted. I don't know what else WEC could have done. Perhaps if Ken's wife Cec was there I could have shared a lot more. It wasn't an ideal situation."

* * *

Cathy still carries around Helen's reply to her letter, a tattered aerogramme, crowded with tiny, neat writing.

Dear Cathy,
Your letter of 11 July is in front of me, and I have cried.
I tried to read it to my girl friend, Pat Morton, but I just

couldn't — I choked with tears, and so did she. Our hearts go out to you ...

... it would be trite for me to produce pat answers — there are none — but just the deep, deep certainty that our loving Heavenly Father knows all, and He has promised that He will not allow Satan to try you beyond what you are able to bear. Underneath are the everlasting arms. His love does surround you, even when the pain is at its worst ...

When I first reached rock-bottom — and cried out to God in loneliness, horror, almost unbelief that it could be so awful, God tenderly and gently whispered: "Can you thank Me ..." and my heart screamed out "No! No! No!" and he patiently said, "Wait a minute. Can you thank Me for TRUSTING YOU ..."

That was a revolutionary thought. I knew I trusted Him, but had never thought about Him trusting me. It was as though He said, "Of course I could have protected you ... taken you out of this terrible situation ... rescued you from all this horror ... but I thought I could now trust you to go through with Me ... I have a plan and a purpose. I cannot explain to you yet. But this tortured suffering has a goal — there is a reason — can you thank Me for trusting you with this experience, even if I never tell you why?"

It was about 2:00 am — and somehow, I stumbled out, "OK. God — yes — I cannot see how anyone can be blessed or helped; I do not understand You; but if You have a plan which will be helped by my heart being crushed by this load of darkness, evil, sin, wickedness, — OK yes God, THANK YOU for daring to trust me with it." — and do you know, almost instantaneously, inexplicably (humanly speaking) the heartbreaking

*agony seemed flooded by a strange and beautiful light –
and I was deeply conscious of the inestimable
PRIVILEGE of being invited to share in some little
measure in His heartbreak and suffering...*

*Dear Cathy, I don't find it easy to offer this to you –
it is a high and difficult walk He is calling you to. BUT
IT IS WITH HIM and He will never fail you or desert
you or let you down.*

"To me that was revolutionary," Cathy said. "That
God trusted me in this situation. He trusted me to
respond in the right way. It was a privilege to
suffer for Jesus and He trusted me with it ... so it
really was a very encouraging letter."

* * *

WEC told Cathy very clearly that she did not need
to go back to Trincomalee, ever.

And, at first, Cathy had no urge to return. "I
think I would have very much liked to have gone
home and said, 'Forget it,' " said Cathy. "I was
fed up.

"But, it went against everything ... I'd been
sitting there for the last so many years, preaching
forgiveness, telling the people that they needed
to learn to love each other. And if I ran away,
what did that say? How can I teach one thing and
not live it?

"Someone once told me an illustration. You

know in Scripture it says we 'will soar on wings like eagles?'[1] They were telling me that when a storm is coming, an eagle will fly towards the storm. The wind pushes him above the clouds. I've always remembered that. If I want to 'soar on wings like eagles,' I have to fly into the storm. If we run away, we'll never get over the problem.

"So I had to go back, to heal myself. If I was going to get rid of that anger, the sin in my life, the unforgiveness, I had to go back and allow God to put on the heat to make the pure gold."

* * *

"Basically I went back in faith," she explained.

"I think an important thing is being honest. I knew I was angry, full of distrust: sinning. I knew I had these things in my life and I knew they were wrong. I had admitted them to God and I'd said, 'God, there's no way I can get rid of these on my own. I'm handing them over to You.'

"God commands us to forgive. He doesn't say, 'if you feel like it.' He commands it. And God will never give us a command that we can't obey. Therefore I knew, without any shadow of doubt, that I was going to be able to forgive. I knew. I didn't know how, but I knew I was.

"I think that's where people get all bogged

---

1. Isaiah 40:31.

down. They don't really believe the word of God. They say they do; but if they really did, they would act on it. When people are terribly hurt, God promises to heal. But people don't believe that. They say 'yes' but act the opposite.

"So I went back and told people, this is the way I am feeling, but I serve a living God and the word of God tells me I have to do this, therefore, somehow, He's going to do it. I'm not going to do it, He's going to do it. I've already told Him I can't."

* * *

There were horrible setbacks.

Cathy had known Nimal since her first day at Fort Frederick. He was one of the handful of Sinhalese Christians she had met in the refugee camp. Thoughtful and gentle, he had always gone out of his way to help her and was like a younger brother to her.

Back in Trincomalee, Cathy met Nimal in a refugee camp.

"Do you know your people took all my things, Nimal? Do you know how that makes me feel?"

He avoided her eyes and said quietly, "I'm sorry, Cathy."

"It really hurts," she told him.

"I'm sorry."

Half an hour later, Cathy talked to a neighbour

who told her about Nimal's own loss during the troubles. His brother-in-law, a policeman, had been taken by the Tamils, tied up and burnt alive. Nimal's sister, not long married, and pregnant, was now a widow at the age of 17.

Horrified, Cathy rushed back to Nimal and begged forgiveness for her hard words; then she went to visit the family.

* * *

"Learning to forgive was," Cathy said, "a slow process. We live in an instantaneous society and we think that if something doesn't happen immediately then God's not going to do it.

"Compare my small amount of suffering with the sufferings of the Sri Lankan Christians. I mean, I lost everything I owned. But how much was that worth? Maybe $500, if you take all my suitcases, my clothes, my radio. And yet other people lost their whole life-savings. The majority of Christians lost everything.

"And then you have the Christians who watched their spouses die. Others were raped. In that context, my suffering was so small. Yet I could see just from the little things that I suffered, how much hatred and anger and unforgiveness was in my heart."

She worked on what she had learnt years before:

"The act of forgiving is when, if you've done something against me, I no longer treat you according to what you've done to me. I treat you in a loving way instead. I may not trust you (trust is a different thing from forgiveness) but I treat you in a caring way, and I don't keep bringing up what you did against me.

"Now I can act that way without feeling it in my heart. But as we act that out, God begins to work in our hearts. If we wait for hearts to change before we act, then we'll never act.

"Normal instinct is to want to retaliate against the hurt that is done against us or against someone we love. And it's just like a volleyball game, the retaliation back and forth.

"But as I acted out what God commanded, God slowly began to change my feelings. I began to see forgiveness in my heart for people and for what they had done.

"And an understanding came. We can very easily say: 'God commands us to forgive', 'hatred is wrong'. We can say all those things and we know it's true. But it's not easy to do. And I empathize with the people who've had to live through that. It is possible to forgive. But it is only possible through God. It is not possible any other way. And without God changing hearts there is no solution to the ethnic problems of this world."

7: "Our God is a God who walks with us"

Cathy worked through these things for two years after the riot.

At the same time, Trincomalee once more settled down into its fragile peace. More local nurses were willing to come to the town so the need for expatriate medical staff was no longer acute.

Cathy began to feel restless. The church among the Sinhalese started to grow rapidly – in Trincomalee and, in separate movements, right across the island. In Trincomalee the Sinhalese Assembly of God church recruited a full-time local pastor. None of this made Cathy superfluous, but she still felt restless.

"I began to feel, 'What am I doing here?' I was handing over my work and thinking, 'What can I do now?' And I feel very strongly that I should not be doing anything that a national can do. I'm there to help them to do it, not to do it myself.

"I could have found plenty to do. But every time I prayed about something I didn't get the go-ahead."

Cathy had asked Ken Booth to keep her in touch with what WEC was doing in South-East Asia. In early 1992, he wrote to say that WEC was thinking about starting work in Cambodia.

Was she interested? In August of that year Ken and Cec visited Cathy and they talked it through.

By now Cathy was also feeling that the work God wanted to do in her in Sri Lanka was over. She had made her peace with the Sinhalese. She had worked through the challenge to forgive and she had seen others take hold of the same principles. God had worked things in her that were not there before the riots of 12 June 1990.

Via the Trincomalee gossip grapevine, she heard that some of the local Christians sometimes said to each other, "If Cathy can learn to forgive, so can we."

"Also," she said, "after the whole situation, when I preached about unforgiveness, hatred, and letting God heal, they listened, because they knew I'd experienced what I was talking about."

* * *

At a WEC regional conference in Bangkok, Thailand, in December 1992, Cathy was able to explore possible placements in Cambodia. Because WEC was not yet registered in that country, WECers were being seconded to other mission groups. Cathy met people from Youth With A Mission (YWAM) who were doing medical work in the north. She was already half-persuaded to go. After talking to the YWAM people she was sure:

"It was just so clear ... everything they wanted in a person, I was, and everything that I desired to do, they were doing. It was so clear ..." So she went back to Sri Lanka, closed up her work, hugged her friends and Tamil family, and left for four months' home leave in the United States.

* * *

With nearly all her working life spent in Asia, Cathy found that America was no longer home. Her church had a new pastor, and *Abba's children* were scattered. It was good to see some friends and family, but she no longer belonged.

"Previously I'd always thought I have somewhere to go back to, somewhere where I could be myself. But I don't feel like that any more," she explained. "Nowhere's home, now. Or, where I am, that's home. And heaven. That's my real home."

* * *

While Cathy was speaking in churches in the United States, the Cambodian nation was slowly waking from its nightmare past. The UN was brokering a peace and elections were being prepared. Long-term humanitarian aid was coming in. Cambodia was returning to something like normality after its freakish, suffering years.

Destablised through the US/Vietnam war, Cambodia had lost one million of its original seven million population under the four-year rule of the Khmer Rouge. Today you can walk through fields where every shovelful of earth yields splinters of human remains. Cambodia's jungles, unlike those of Sri Lanka, are quiet: the Buddhist Khmer people hunted the wildlife to extinction in the desperate famine years between 1974 and 1979.

The Khmer Rouge tide carried off 9,000 of the 10,000 Christians, nearly all the Buddhist monks; and most of the people who could read, who had any kind of education, or who even had the bad luck to own a pair of glasses. An invasion in 1979 replaced the hated Khmer Rouge with the even-more-despised Vietnamese. These invaders finally left in 1989.

The years of war left a climate of fear and distrust hanging over the land and ten million dinner-plate-sized green landmines buried in the fertile rice fields. The Khmer Rouge still run a portion of the country. By every measure of human development Cambodia ranked with the least and the worst nations in the United Nations intensive care ward.

About 700,000 Cambodians fled the country during the Khmer Rouge years. Perhaps half of them were given refugee status and have had a better time of it. Many have prospered in countries such as the United States and France and a number have turned to Christ.

* * *

Cathy's speaking schedule took her to two Cambodian churches in Atlanta. She shared with them how she was going to do public health education up in the little northern province of Stoeng Tréng, where no-one went, close to the border with Laos.

Afterwards, she met a shy, middle-aged Cambodian named Kham. He was from Stoeng Tréng. He had not seen his mother or brothers and sisters since he fled Cambodia in 1974. He had become a Christian in 1985 and for seven years had been praying for his family and writing to them, sometimes sharing about Jesus. One of his relatives had written back: "We would like to know more about this but there's no-one here to teach us."

Cathy explains: "After Kham told me his story, neither of us had any doubt that I was the answer to those years of prayer. Kham and his church were ecstatic. And for me ... even though I already knew God was calling me to Cambodia, this was just like an extra seal, like something special was going to happen. Something marvellous was in the works. God was going to do something."

* * *

After flying in to Cambodia, Cathy spent just one month in the capital, Phnom Penh with its grand, tattered French colonial buildings, potholed roads, masses of children, electricity wires in all directions, infant hopes and bleak shadows. Then she headed up to Stoeng Tréng.

She carried with her some letters for Kham's relatives. Accompanying her for a week, to help her settle in, was a bilingual girl friend, Allie.

On day two in Stoeng Tréng, Cathy and Allie went to the market. "I had letters from Kham to his aunt and to his mother," Cathy remembers. "I had no idea how I was going to find these people. There are not, you know, street addresses. I had two names, and the names of two villages." So they thought they might get some clues in the market.

"Oh yes," said the first stallholder they tried. "That's my relative." This person went off and that same day, Cathy met Kham's aunt. A week or so later, Kham's mother (a little bald lady) came down the Sekong river from the village of Siempang, which was eight hours away by boat. "Tell Kham to please visit quickly," she said over and over again. "Because I don't know how much longer I'll be alive for him to see."

* * *

Six months was all the situation allowed for language learning. Cathy moved in with a Khmer family in Stoeng Tréng. In the mornings she did language drill with an instructor. In the afternoons, sitting down with the stallholders, she (for the most part) laughed and fooled around trying out her Khmer in the market.

"Six months is definitely not enough time," she decided. But she stuck a Bible verse on her wall – "The one who calls you is faithful and he will do it"[2] – and did her best. When you read Khmer, vowels can be before the consonant, above the consonant, behind the consonant, or below the consonant. There are no spaces between words, and lots of silent letters, like the 'h's in Phnom Penh. So reading is like doing a big jigsaw or word search puzzle.

In January 1993 she started work. Her role in the YWAM Stoeng Tréng team – alongside three other nurses and a married couple – was to produce public health education programmes. They would be aimed at two groups: the government nurses, one or two of whom are assigned to each cluster of villages; and the schoolteachers. In this way the whole province could receive teaching on basic preventative health care. Parallel programmes were organized by the team in areas such as immunizing children, maternal care and malaria control.

* * *

2. 1 Thessalonians 5:24.

In their spare time, the team saw people coming to Christ, both in Stoeng Tréng town and beyond. Old and young, middle-class and dirt-poor, sometimes in whole families, people were turning to Jesus. As many as 40 worshipped in the Stoeng Tréng house church started by the team.

According to Cathy quite a number in Stoeng Tréng "were just sitting there waiting to hear about Jesus. The girl who lived next door came to me and said, 'I hear you're a Christian. I want to follow Jesus too.'"

Another lady had gone to Catholic Sunday School as a child. She came to them: "I believe Jesus is God, and I want to follow Him." They gave her some Bible studies to do, she did them, and then said, "I'm ready. I've done the questions and I believe it and I want to follow."

A young boy came up to the YWAM leader carrying a handwritten note in English, saying, "Please tell me about Jesus." He had been hearing the gospel from Christian radio.

In January 1994, for a few precious days, Kham visited. All the family except his mother cried when they saw him. "I won't cry," she said. "Because if I do my tears will wash him away again."

Kham's visit tied in with a local immunization and education programme organized by the team. A little later, a couple of Kham's relatives turned to Christ, the first fruits of his years of prayer.

A few months later still, Kham's nephew came to visit, also from the United States. A gifted worship leader in both Khmer and English, he greatly strengthened the church. Twenty people were baptized shortly before he left.

The response of Cambodians to the gospel is surprising everyone. Cathy says:

"I feel like I'm on holy ground ... What God is doing here, and that God should choose to use me, to be even a small part of it, I feel so overwhelmed...

"And it's not us. It's God. People we would not even think about are coming to the Lord. We're not seeking them out; they're seeking us out.

"And to know that I'm an answer to Kham's prayer is very humbling. It could make me proud, but it's also very humbling. The prayers of that church in Atlanta are sweet smelling incense to God, because their prayers are so in earnest, so in depth. I think God is hearing them and doing a marvellous work."

* * *

The church has had setbacks. There have been pastoral problems. There were three Christian funerals in the first six months of the church's life. People were asking around the town, "Does someone in your family have to die when you become a Christian?" Distrust bred by years of communism and war is sometimes still apparent in people's minds. And while they have seen one or two miraculous healings, more often their prayers for the sick have just tumbled into the void.

Cathy notes: "I think people do see a change in those who are coming to Christ. They're seeing that our God is a God who walks with us through all the problems. Because the congregation is having the same problems as they're having. They're sick, they have money problems, they don't have enough to eat, people in their family are dying, and yet they're full of joy. I think that's been a big example."

* * *

No-one knows how long this Cambodian springtime is going to last. Or if it's springtime at all. Few would bet on the country's long-term stability.

For Cathy, this is where God has put her. She does not want to go anywhere else for the rest of her life and her spirit is satisfied.

"I feel that Malaysia and Sri Lanka were training grounds. God did use me, but I feel that both of those were preparation for where I am right now. I loved Sri Lanka, and its people, but I never had the complete satisfaction that I feel right now in Cambodia."

The insights into forgiveness, the practical experiences, everything has fitted Cathy for the ministry in Cambodia at this unique time. Normally she follows God step by step, day by day, but just occasionally she glimpses the grand panorama. She remembers that time back in nursing school when God spoke to her audibly, saying He was going to use her in mighty way.

"I believe that, no matter what's happened in the past, and no matter what's going to happen in the future, where I am right now, in Cambodia, that promise is going to be fulfilled."

She sees all the past as the apprenticeship, the equipping. That's why she is excited about the future.

"There are just so many coincidences ... experience for over ten years in Asian medicine and diseases ... having worked in a government system so similar, and yet so advanced ... having worked and dealt with all the problems of refugees ... having helped to develop a medical system for villages. It's like God has been preparing me for this medical work.

"There's the coincidence with Kham and the church there and them praying for me. That I would meet his aunt, that I would be right there, that Kham and then his nephew would be able to come. All of these things, fitting together like a puzzle that has just been dropped out of heaven and all the pieces falling into the right place.

"I love God's coincidences! And I've never felt God's anointing on me as I do now. I have never felt as satisfied — even with all the problems — in what I'm doing. My spirit confirms to me that God is doing something marvellous and all the circumstances confirm it as well."

* * *

But he said to me, 'My grace is sufficient for you, for my power is made perfect in weakness.' Therefore I will boast all the more gladly about my weaknesses, so that Christ's power may rest on me. That is why, for Christ's sake, I delight in weaknesses, in insults, in hardships, in persecutions, in difficulties. For when I am weak, then I am strong (1 Corinthians 12:9, 10).

To find out more about serving the Lord
with WEC please contact:

WEC International
(Australia)
48 Woodside Avenue
Strathfield
NSW 2135
Australia

WEC International
(New Zealand)
PO Box 27-264
Mt. Roskill
Auckland 1030
New Zealand

WEC International
(Britain)
Bulstrode
Oxford Road
Gerrards Cross
Bucks
SL9 8SZ
UK

WEC International
(Singapore)
PO Box 185
Raffles City
Singapore 911707

WEC International
(South Africa)
PO Box 47777
Greyville 4023
Republic of South Africa

WEC International
(Canada)
37 Aberdeen Avenue
Hamilton
Ontario L8P 2N6
Canada

WEC International (USA)
PO Box 1707
Fort Washington
PA 19034
USA

WEC International
(Hong Kong)
PO Box 73261
Kowloon Central Post
Office
Kowloon
Honk Kong

Contact WEC USA if you
want to keep with news of
Cathy's ministry.